RANGER RICK'S BEST FRIENDS

HI, I'M RANGER RICK, the official con-
servation symbol for young members of
the National Wildlife Federation, and
leader of the Ranger Rick Nature Clubs.
On behalf of all the animals in Deep
Green Wood, welcome to our world of
nature and wildlife.

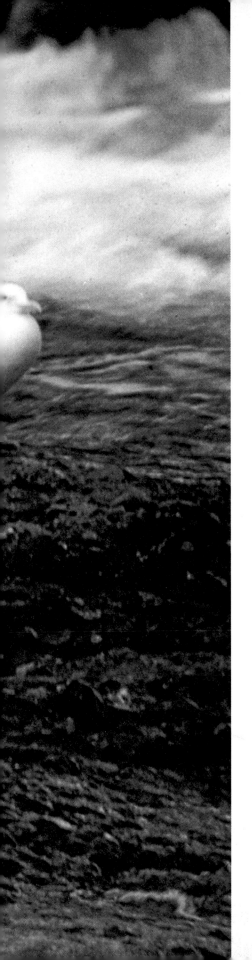

The Big Bears

by Fred Johnson

**Created and Produced by
The National Wildlife Federation
Washington, D. C.**

1 Ranger Rick Visits the Park Bears

by J.A. Brownridge

Ranger Rick, Cubby Bear, and Ollie Otter had traveled way out West to visit Cubby's Cousin Willy, who lived in Yellowstone National Park. They had just entered the park and were admiring the hugh snow-capped mountains and the beautiful green forests. As they rounded a grove of trees, Rick stopped.

"Look over there at the roadway."

"What a terrific traffic jam!" exclaimed Cubby. A long line of cars stood still on the hill. Horns were honking and radiators were boiling over. "Probably there was an accident. Let's see!"

When they reached the first car in the traffic jam, Rick and his friends could see two black bears standing in the middle of the road. Gathered around them was a happy group of people taking pictures. Some were giving the bears food, and some were even putting their arms around the big wild animals. Sitting up in a tree above the excitement were two little black bear cubs who had learned to head for high timber in a commotion.

"Those people should leave the bears alone!" Rick said as he and Ollie and Cubby reached the edge of the crowd. "Bears can get angry and dangerous!"

"Look what's happening now," Ollie pointed out. A man had pulled a third curious bear into the circle; the bear sat down, panting heavily in the summer heat. Then the man picked up his little son, no more than four or five years old, and tried to put him on the bear's back so he could take a picture.

"Oh my gosh, that's Cousin Willie!" Cubby cried. "And those two little ones up in the tree are his cubs. Willie's a very nice bear, but he isn't going to like all that pushing and pulling. What do they think he is, a circus bear? He's wild—just like all the other animals out here at Yellowstone!"

So he and Ollie and Rick ran into the middle of the crowd and tried to separate bears from people. They urged the bears back into the forest and the people back into their cars. But before the cars started moving again, a blood-curdling scream came from an open window. Rick dashed down the hill and saw a growling, angry bear reaching into a car, his big claws just missing the faces of the frightened people.

Willie arrived in time to deliver a strong down-field block. The other bear went away with an angry snarl.

"The people had been teasing him with food," Willie explained later. "He was really just trying to get what had been promised him. No wonder he was mean and mad."

"Does this go on all summer?" Rick asked. It was now nighttime, and the friends were sitting around their Yellowstone campfire talking over the first day's events.

"It sure does," Willie said, "You'd think people would be smarter."

"But why do they have to throw around so many tin cans and so much junk?" Cubby asked.

"And why don't they get out and walk, and enjoy the beautiful sights of the park instead of just sitting in their automobiles?" Ollie added.

"I don't know. People are funny," Willie concluded with a shrug.

"Hey, now—come on," Rick said. "Let's get on our feet ourselves and go look at the park. That's why we're here.

"That's right," said Willie. "Let me show you guys around. This is the best time—when the moon's up and the people are asleep. Would you like to see some of our 3000 geysers, waterfalls, or hot springs?"

"What's a geyser?" Ollie asked as they padded down the trail.

"Well, you know—like 'Old Faithful,'" Willie began to explain. But before he could say more, they had reached a low log fence. "Hey, don't go in there!" he called to Ollie, who had raced on ahead.

"Oh, don't worry," Ollie called back. "There's nothing in here but a hole in the ground. I'll be careful."

Suddenly, before he had time to jump back, the hole erupted. A huge column of water and steam shot into the air. Ollie went head over heels, landing in a heap at the feet of his friends.

"Somebody just fired an underground rocket!" he gasped. "Let's get out of here." When they saw he wasn't hurt, the animals laughed at Ollie, who was still so frightened his smooth hair stood right up on end.

"That wasn't a rocket," said Willie. "That was 'Old Faithful' geyser. It does that right on schedule almost every hour. There are many geysers, as I told you, but none puts on its show so regularly as this one. Let's go see some more of the park, but be sure to stay on the trails and obey the danger signs."

Off in the distance they could hear a

rumble, like thunder. As they got closer, the sound got louder and louder until they could hardly hear each other. Then, around a bend, they saw in the moonlight the great Yellowstone Falls.

"My gracious, that's beautiful," Rick shouted above the roaring water.

Willie's two cubs were playing along the bank, wrestling and tumbling happily. Suddenly one of them tripped and fell into the river with a splash!

Without stopping to think, Ollie dove in after him. He knew bears could swim, but he also knew that the little one was no match for that strong current.

Swiftly he swam after the floundering cub who was being swept toward the edge of the falls. He grabbed for him and missed. On the next try he got hold of him, but though they both tried, they made no progress toward shore.

Ollie was slowly losing his grip on the struggling, slippery cub. Just when all seemed lost, the two animals were swept near a low-hanging branch. With a last desperate effort, Ollie stretched out and caught it.

"Help!" he gasped. "I can't hold on!"

Rick rushed out on the branch. Quickly he pulled Ollie closer until he could drag the cub to safety.

Freed of his heavy burden, Ollie struggled out of the water and over to his grateful friends. After all that excitement everyone decided to rest for a while.

During the next few days and nights Rick, Ollie, and Cubby saw many wonderful things in Yellowstone. They also saw that the Park Rangers were doing everything they could to stop people from feeding the bears or leaving food and garbage out in the open for the bolder animals. Some people who wouldn't learn were arrested; some bears who kept invading the campgrounds were taken farther off into the wilderness by helicopter "bearlifts."

At last it was time for the three friends to start back home. As they were leaving the park, Rick realized he had an important message for his friends.

"Please, Rangers, if you go to the park and see a bear, look at it, enjoy it, but stay away from it, and practice good outdoor manners at your campsites."

7

2 When a Black Bear Wakes Up

Imagine being born outdoors in February during a howling blizzard! Two black bear cubs were.

Their mother was in the middle of her long winter sleep. Her den was a hollowed-out place under some big rocks covered with snow. Sometimes the icy wind blew snow between the rocks, but this bear family did not feel the cold. Mother had three inches of fat under her thick winter coat. She was able to keep her newborn cubs warm and snug in her soft fur.

Let's call the cubs Barney and Betsy. Each weighed only nine ounces when born. Mother weighed 300 pounds.

For the next month the cubs slept, nursed, and grew. How they grew! By the middle of March each weighed three pounds and was about 13 inches long. And then came one warm day in April when their mother coaxed the two fat little cubs outside.

Snug in a den, the black bear settles down to sleep during the cold winter months. Sometimes he wakes up *(left)* and comes out to look around.

A black bear cub soon learns to climb a tree. He waits until danger is past.

In the sunlight Barney looked black, but Betsy was light brown. This was not unusual because black bears often come in different colors.

At first the cubs were confused by the strange smells, sounds, and sights. They had to find out what each new thing was. Everything had to be tasted and sniffed.

The cubs watched while mother ate grasses and twigs, pine bark and ants, and beetles and mice. Then they tried some, too.

The whole world seemed one big playground to them. They quickly learned to go up a tree faster than you or I could. Coming down was something else. They just slid down and let go a few feet from the bottom. How they landed didn't seem to matter.

Boxing, wrestling, and just plain snooping around took up a lot of time. If they got too far from mother she went after them and gave them a swat. They quickly forgot and were into some other mischief.

Splashing in a nearby stream was great fun and mother showed them how to grab a frog for a snack. It was fun, too, to rip rotten logs apart and slurp up the fat grubs and termites. Twice they found a wild bee colony in an old dead tree and feasted on the honey.

And so until late fall the cubs played and learned, ate and got fatter and fatter. One day something cold, wet, and white fell from the sky. It was time to look for a place to sleep through the winter snow.

Not long after, mother found a den in the side of a bank and began to enlarge it by digging. The cubs helped. This year they would den with mother, but next year they would find their own. In the spring mother would chase them away to survive on their own.

During the hot days of summer, a black bear like Barney tries to keep cool. He has a regular bathing hole, just as you do. He loves to swim and can swim five miles without stopping. Sometimes he finds a muddy pool and just wallows in the mud.

Bears will eat almost everything. In the picture above one happily munches a bee comb, for wild honey is a special treat. A bear pays no attention to angry bees. His fur coat is too heavy for bees to get through, and stings on his nose don't seem to bother him.

Garbage cans in bear country will attract bears. The bears smell the food and will go to any lengths to get it. Following the scent, they will come right into campgrounds, nosing into refuse heaps or trash cans. Do you think this fat bear can get out of the can he has discovered?

3 The Really Big American Bears

he black bear is big,
he polar bear *(left)*
nd grizzly bear *(right)*
re bigger, but the
rown bear is the
iggest bear of all.

Grizzly Bear

The Grizzly was once "King of the American Wilderness." Other animals fled when he approached. Early pioneers, farmers, trappers, and Indians told countless stories of his ferocious disposition and fierce fighting ability.

Even his scientific name is enough to frighten you: *Ursus horribilis!*

Actually the grizzly usually leads a rather solitary life and is aggressive only when something or someone starts snooping around his "backyard." A female grizzly with her cubs is particularly dangerous when something gets too close.

Each of the grizzly's forepaws is at least the size of your head and has five thick 6-inch claws. His weight can be between 350 and 850 pounds. When an adult male grizzly stands on his hind legs, he may be 8 feet tall. Because of his light outer fur and grizzled appearance, he is sometimes called "Silver Tip."

In spite of his great bulk, the grizzly is very fast. He can outrun a horse in rough country. And reports of his strength are not exaggerated. He has been seen to break the neck of a 500-pound steer with one blow and then carry it off without effort.

Grizzlies rarely kill healthy adult large animals, but they feast upon deer, antelope, elk, and cows killed by cold weather. After eating, grizzlies bury what is left for another day.

They also enjoy grasses, bulbs, berries, grubs, squirrels, gophers, and fish.

Once the frontiersmen fought the grizzly. Today man fights to save the few of these magnificent beasts that remain in the American wilderness.

Grizzlies live in high rolling meadows with thickets for shade and cover.

Brown Bear

This monster is the "Big Daddy" of the bear world. He is the largest land-dwelling meat-eater in the world.

Like all bears, his hearing and smelling senses are extremely sharp but his eyesight is poor. So, when he suspects that something is approaching, he stands up on his hind legs to try and see better. He stands up, and up, and up, until he may tower more than 11 feet! If he were to spread his "arms," his gigantic front paws, each the size of a basketball, would be 8 or 9 feet apart.

It is strange to see these huge creatures grazing like cows. But they do, at times. Sweet grasses, plants, and berries all help to nourish their 1600-pound bodies. Small rodents make a welcome snack, and whenever the bears can, they like to fish.

From June to October the swift-flowing Alaskan streams are filled with spawning salmon, the bears' richest food source. Groups of hungry bears gather along the banks and fish in favorite spots for hours.

The brown bear has other names. One is the Kodiak Bear. Another is the Alaskan Brown Bear. And finally he is called the Big Brown Bear. Can you see why?

He stands up to watch other bears. Like them, he tries to scoop the fish from the water and to catch them in his mouth. But the fish move faster than he can. Now he is hungry and tired. Perhaps he can rest in the sun before trying again.

What's that wiggling flash? Without thinking, he pounces. Success! The biggest fish of all!

It's July and salmon fishing time! Last year this young brown bear cub waited for mother to bring his food. Now he must catch his own.

He is very excited—but also confused. He sits in the water, watching the fish swim right past him. How are you supposed to catch them? He swats carelessly at the fish, then faster and faster, and with both paws. No luck.

Polar Bear

Sometimes called the ''Ghost of the North,'' this big bear spends its entire life roaming over the land of ice and snow.

Polar bears are big. Standing up they may be 10 feet high and weigh up to 1600 pounds. They have a longer neck and smaller head than other bears, and the small black nose tip is about the size of a softball. Their broad feet have nonskid, hairy soles; they can walk, run, and climb on ice.

King of the Arctic, a polar bear strides across the ice.

They are strong swimmers and have been seen paddling along as far out as 100 miles at sea. More often, though, if they decide to change their hunting ground they "thumb a ride" on a passing ice floe. Their dense underfur keeps the frigid arctic water from their skin. A thick 3-inch layer of fat also protects them from cold.

Polar bears never cease to wander and hunt, both on land and water. For a few months in late spring they can fill up with moss, grasses, seaweed, and berries. But most of the year nothing grows in this Arctic region, so the big white bears must eat meat.

Seals are the main prey of these skillful hunters. A polar bear may lie and wait beside a seal's breathing hole in the ice. Or he may stalk the seal, taking advantage of his white coat to remain invisible by each mound of snow. He moves only when the seal is not looking. Then, when he gets close enough, he moves with surprising swiftness.

Two cubs go along for the ice-floe ride when mother goes hunting for seals.

The bear's yellowish-white fur blends well with the snow and ice, but what about that fat black nose tip? Hunters and Eskimos both report that polar bears have been seen to put a shaggy front paw over his nose to hide the black tip while waiting a chance to move forward!

The arctic world is harsh. Only the strong survive. Polar bear cubs face a difficult life from the moment they are born in midwinter in a hollow dug in a snow bank. Like all bear cubs, they watch mother and learn quickly. For perhaps two years they feed on mother's prey. Then she chases them off.

Polar bears have no natural enemies except man. Eskimo hunters kill this bear for practical survival needs. Its meat supplies food for many families for a long time. The tanned hide is used for waterproof boats, sleeping bags, sled covers, and shelters. With the fur still on and worn inside, the pelt becomes warm clothing and boots. Bone splinters become needles; sinews become thread. The teeth and claws are used for pegs or scrapers, and even for decorative jewelry.

No wonder the Eskimos are grateful for the polar bear and call him Nanook, the Big Fellow.

by J.A. Brownridge

It was the middle of summer, but a cold wind was blowing across the ice fields in the far North. Ranger Rick and his friend Ollie Otter shivered as they stood on the ice. The two friends had traveled far from home into this cold country to visit Cubby Bear's Cousin Wilbur, the polar bear.

Gray, frigid water stretched before them as far as their eyes could see. Huge cliffs of glacial ice rose steeply above the water.

Rick stopped suddenly with his nose in the air. He sniffed, then peered around intently. He looked worried and puzzled.

"I smell something, Ollie, but I sure can't see anything," he said.

Slowly and carefully they moved on, eyes squinting against the glare of the sun on the snow.

"We've been waiting for you!" A deep voice seemed to come from right beside them in the white silence.

Snow and ice flew in all directions as Rick and Ollie leaped in fright and started to run.

"Hey, wait a minute," boomed the deep voice reassuringly. "It's only me—Wilbur, the polar bear—the one you've come to visit."

Rick and Ollie paused in their flight. Sure enough, they could just make out a big, white form. It had blended in so well with the snow they hadn't even noticed his black nose.

4 Ranger Rick Adrift on an Iceberg

"Wow," gasped Ollie, "I sure thought somebody had us that time. I guess our eyes aren't used to all this snow and icy glare."

Wilbur's hearty laugh boomed out. "Up here a lot of the animals and birds are white like the snow they live on. I'm sure glad to see you. Let's go over to my home so you can get some food and rest a while."

Off they trotted. Wilbur lumbered along, looking very clumsy but moving with a speed that was surprising for such a huge animal. They soon came to a big cave that had been made into a

den for Wilbur's family. His mate and two cubs greeted them warmly. Rick and Ollie were glad to be in out of the wind and were soon happily exchanging stories about their animal friends.

"You're so big and hard to see. I guess you don't have to worry about any enemies," said Ollie enviously.

"Don't you believe it," replied Wilbur sadly. "Our biggest problem is that we *are* so big and have such nice fur. For a while we were hunted from airplanes, ships, and icemobiles. And in some areas we were in danger of disappearing. But now conservationists have

wide for us to jump and it is much too cold for us to swim in."

At that moment, the friendly head of Wilbur popped up over the side of the iceberg.

"Well," laughed Wilbur reassuringly. "You're getting a free boat ride, I see."

"I don't think it's funny," growled Ollie. "How are we going to get off? It's easy for you. You're used to this cold water, but Rick and I would become two chunks of ice if we tried to swim."

"Hold tight," laughed Wilbur. And with that, he and his family, swimming in the ice-cold water just as Ollie would have done in Shady Pond, began pushing the floating piece of ice slowly and carefully back toward the mainland.

"How do you like your own private raft with its four-bear-power motor?" asked Wilbur.

WHERE BEARS LIVE

POLAR BEARS roam the polar regions at the top of the world. In North America they visit lands touched by the Arctic Seas—the northern shores of Labrador, Canada, and Alaska.

GRIZZLY BEARS are seen in Wyoming, Montana, and Idaho. Most are in Yellowstone and Glacier National Parks. In the north they range wooded mountains of the Canadian Rockies and into Alaska.

BLACK BEARS, the bears of many colors, are found in the woodland areas of the East and the swamps of the South. From central Mexico through the Rocky Mountains into Canada and Alaska.

black phase

blue phase

cinnamon phase

BROWN BEARS live on a narrow strip along the Pacific Coast stretching from British Columbia to the Alaskan Peninsula. Also on numerous off-shore islands such as Kodiak and Admiralty.

31

WHEN YOU SEE A BEAR . . .

Notice his flatfooted, shuffling gait. He ambles along on the soles of his feet, just as we do. Some American Indians even called the bear "beasts that walk like man." Look at his size: his stocky body is like a barrel and his thick, strong legs appear too short. The thick shaggy fur almost covers a tiny tail.

The bear may be seen at any time. He eats all day long at an unhurried rate, and can find something to eat just about anywhere. He sleeps whenever and wherever he chooses.

Watch for the black bear in forested wilderness areas such as the mountains of West Virginia and Pennsylvania and the National Parks. He is often seen in the Great Smoky Mountain, Yellowstone, Grand Teton, and Glacier National Parks. In some parks bears beg food from passing cars. They stand on their back legs and "wave." The people then stop and try to feed the bears. This is extremely dangerous.

Remember that this friendly-looking animal with the playful cubs is WILD. The bear looks like a tame pet or huge toy, but actually he is a big and powerful wild creature. Do not feed the bear, get too close to him, or try to tease him. The best way to enjoy the park bear is to look at him through your closed car windows and leave him alone. It's more fun to watch his natural actions than those brought about by hunger for man's food.

CREDITS

C. Kent Armstrong black bear cover; Steve McCutcheon brown bear cubs pages 2-3, 17; Willis Peterson 8; John J. Craighead 9; John Akela, Full Moon Studio 10; Leonard Lee Rue III 11, 20, 21; Dr. E. R. Degginger 12; Leonard Lee Rue IV 13 top; George F. Stover 13 bottom; George H. Harrison 14, 16, 25; Tom Myers 15, 18; Cecil Rhode 19; Dr. Martin W. Schein 22-23; Thor Larsen, World Wildlife Fund 24; Gene C. Frazier 32; Karl Maslowski back cover. Drawings by Frank Fretz 30-31.

NATIONAL WILDLIFE FEDERATION

Thomas L. Kimball	*Executive Vice President*
J. A. Brownridge	*Administrative Vice President*
James D. Davis	*Book Development*

Staff for This Book

EDITOR	Russell Bourne
ASSOCIATE EDITOR	Bonnie S. Lawrence
ART DIRECTOR	Donna M. Sterman
ART ASSISTANT	Ellen Robling
RANGER RICK ADVENTURES	J. A. Brownridge
RANGER RICK ART	Lorin Thompson
COPY EDITOR	Virginia R. Rapport
PRODUCTION AND PRINTING	Jim DeCrevel
	Mel M. Baughman, Jr.
CONSULTANT	Edwin Gould, Ph.D
	The Johns Hopkins University

OUR OBJECTIVES

To encourage the intelligent management of the life-sustaining resources of the earth—its productive soil, its essential water sources, its protective forests and plantlife, and its dependent wildlife—and to promote and encourage the knowledge and appreciation of these resources, their interrelationship and wise use, without which there can be little hope for a continuing abundant life.